A Symphony of Color

A Symphony

First Church in Cambridge, Congregational, United Church of Christ

Cambridge, Massachusetts

# of Color

Stained Glass at First Church

Patricia H. Rodgers

Photographs by Allen Hess

Dedicated to the Ministers of First Church, and in particular, Allen Happe

Front cover: Hart Window
Inside front cover: Resurrection Angel
Back cover: Angel
Inside back cover: St. Catherine of Alexandria

Copyright © 1990 Patricia H. Rodgers

Library of Congress Catalog Card Number 90-80873

ISBN 0-9626196-0-4

Contents

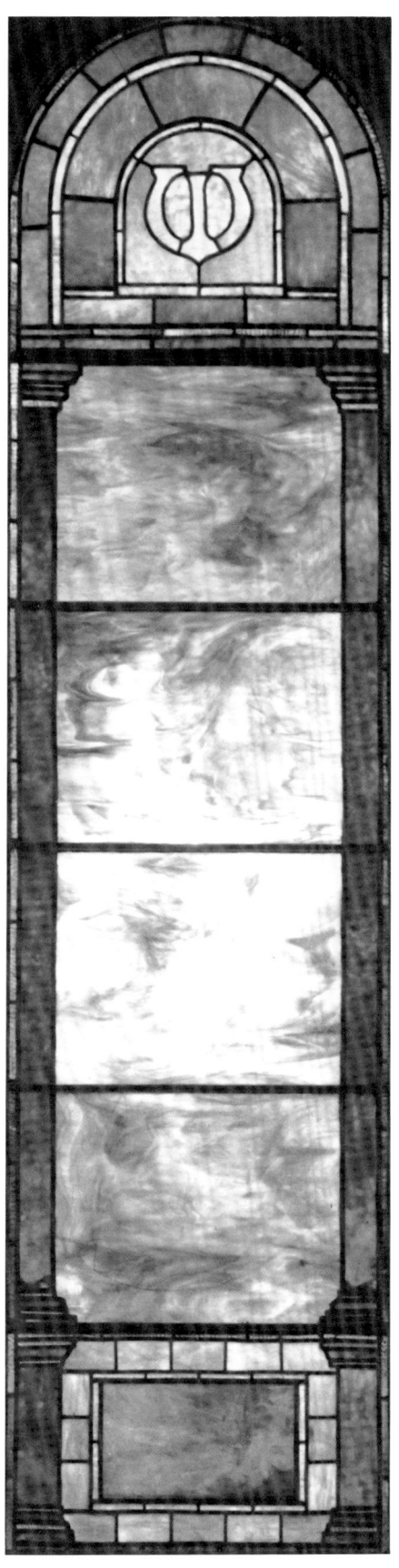

Foreword . . . 6

Preface . . . 6

List of Stained Glass Windows . . . 8

Window Diagram . . . 9

Brief History of the Church . . . 10

Introduction to Stained Glass Windows . . . 15

Guide to the Windows . . . 23

Glossary . . . 56

Donors and Dedications . . . 57

Ministers . . . 58

Stained Glass Studios . . . 58

Architects . . . 61

Bibliography . . . 63

Opalescent Chancel Windows, with alpha and omega symbols (p. 53)

Foreword

This book is a guide to the stained glass that adorns the sixth meetinghouse of the First Church in Cambridge, Congregational, United Church of Christ. Initially, it seemed like a clearly prescribed project. It became an intricate puzzle. Although the glass is intact, many questions about it remained. Fortunately, the author of this study uncovered more information than I thought possible to know about these windows. Her unique emphasis is on the people who commissioned them, the people for whom they were given, and the studios that produced them.

The windows of First Church do not belong to a comprehensive scheme nor to a single style, subject or studio. They are a melange. Each must be viewed in its own light. They surround us when we gather with an aura of names, faces, and angels. They also display some of the most exquisite coloration and blending of hues known to any art form. The idea to explore and tell these untold stories arose as the congregation celebrated its 350th anniversary, recalling not only its founding moments but its continuous history as well. Happily, the present congregation commissioned the cleaning and restoration of these windows for the enjoyment and inspiration of worshipers and wayfarers in generations to come.

There was a time in Puritan New England when such adornments would not have been allowed. There was a time more recently when some folks would gladly have thrown them out! Fashions come and go. At present, we are of a mind to appreciate the craft, the beauty, and the stories of these windows. Patricia H. Rodgers has made a major contribution toward our appreciation.

Allen Happe, Pastor

Preface

The 350th anniversary of First Church provided the impetus for writing about its stained glass. For over a century, worshippers and visitors have been surrounded by the multicolored images but known little about them. It seemed an appropriate time to uncover and publish information about the windows, including their origins, designers, and donors.

Without the encouragement of two people in particular, this study would never even have begun. The Pastor of First Church, Allen Happe, enthusiastically supported the idea, while Susan D. Moran, the Parish Administrator, provided invaluable knowledge as well as access to the First Church archives. Both individuals provided crucial, ongoing support, ideas, and encouragement over a period of three years.

What we expected to be a simple task of filling in the missing pieces turned out to be quite the opposite. The endeavor was similar to completing a complicated jigsaw puzzle. Some pieces seemed to fall into place by themselves, others required greater effort, and there always remained large gaps to be filled in. Eventually, we had to concede that some of the pieces would never be found, but in the end we had a much clearer picture than ever before.

Thanks to the efforts of many individuals, information was unearthed in a variety of places. In addition to the staff of First Church, knowledgeable people guided me to appropriate sources at the Harvard Archive, the New England Area Center of the Archives of American Art, Mount Auburn Cemetery, and the Cambridge Public Library. Janice Chadbourne, Curator of the Fine Arts Department of the Boston Public Library, and her staff provided invaluable material about the windows as well as the architectural firms associated with First Church.

Through correspondence with stained glass historians, missing pieces began to appear. Helene Weis, librarian of The Willet Stained Glass Studios, Inc., provided a wealth of material about the Willet windows. Hugh F. McKean, President of the Charles Hosmer Morse Foundation, Inc., shared his knowledge of Tiffany stained glass. Hazel D. O'Malley located archival material relating to the Reynolds, Francis and Rohnstock window.

Technical expertise was provided by a number of stained glass experts, including Alice Johnson and Daniel Maher of the Lyn Hovey Studio. Julie Sloan of McKernan Satterlee Associates provided essential technical knowledge as well as a guide to stained glass terminology. Both Orin Skinner and Marilyn Justice provided insight into little-known facets of the world of stained glass.

Members of the First Church congregation and staff filled in more missing pieces. Peter Sykes, Music Director, provided information about the church's musical history. Richard John and Mac Howland lent assistance in regard to the Horsford family and photographic techniques respectively.

Through the efforts of three people, Allen Hess, Catherine Olofson, and Susan Marsh, the visual and verbal aspects of the book took shape. With skill and patience, Allen Hess photographed the stained glass, revealing a richness of detail previously unnoticed. Catherine Olofson provided invaluable editorial assistance. With an artistic eye, Susan Marsh skillfully combined both photographs and text into a finished work that is greater than the sum of its parts.

My husband, John Ex Rodgers, and friends Olivia Parker and Sarah B. Jolliffe provided invaluable assistance throughout the past three years.

It is my hope that this historical perspective will give observers a heightened awareness, a greater understanding, and a deeper appreciation of the stained glass windows of First Church.

Patricia H. Rodgers

List of Stained Glass Windows

[1] Faith, p. 35
1898
The Tiffany Glass & Decorating Company

[2] They Shall Be Mine, Saith the Lord, p. 30
1895
The Tiffany Glass & Decorating Company

[3] Horsford Rose Window, p. 25
1872
Studio unknown

[4] The Four Elements, p. 29
1895
The Tiffany Glass & Decorating Company

[5] Opalescent Chancel Window, p. 53

[6] Mary of Bethany, p. 44
1957
The Willet Stained Glass Studios, Inc.

[7] Fuller Window, p. 31
1895
Studio unknown

[8] The Good Shepherd, p. 27
1894
The Tiffany Glass & Decorating Company

[9] Angel, p. 32
1895
The Tiffany Glass & Decorating Company

[10] Dorcas, p. 46
1957
The Willet Stained Glass Studios, Inc.

[11] Opalescent Chancel Window, p. 53

[12] Hart Window, p. 36
1901
Studio unknown

[13] Kimball/Rice Window, p. 39
1918 and 1960
Horace J. Phipps and Company
The Willet Stained Glass Studios, Inc.

[14] Resurrection Angel, p. 33
1897
The Tiffany Glass & Decorating Company

[15] St. Paul, p. 34
1898
The Tiffany Glass & Decorating Company

[16] Bancroft Window, p. 42
1929
Reynolds, Francis and Rohnstock

[17] Christ Blessing Little Children, p. 50
1957
The Willet Stained Glass Studios, Inc.

[18] Lester Grisaille Windows, p. 48
1957
The Willet Stained Glass Studios, Inc.

[19] St. Catherine of Alexandria, p. 37
1908
Tiffany Studios

[20] Chapel Windows, p. 52
c. 1939
Arthur Murray Dallin

[*] Small stenciled lunettes, p. 53

Window Diagram

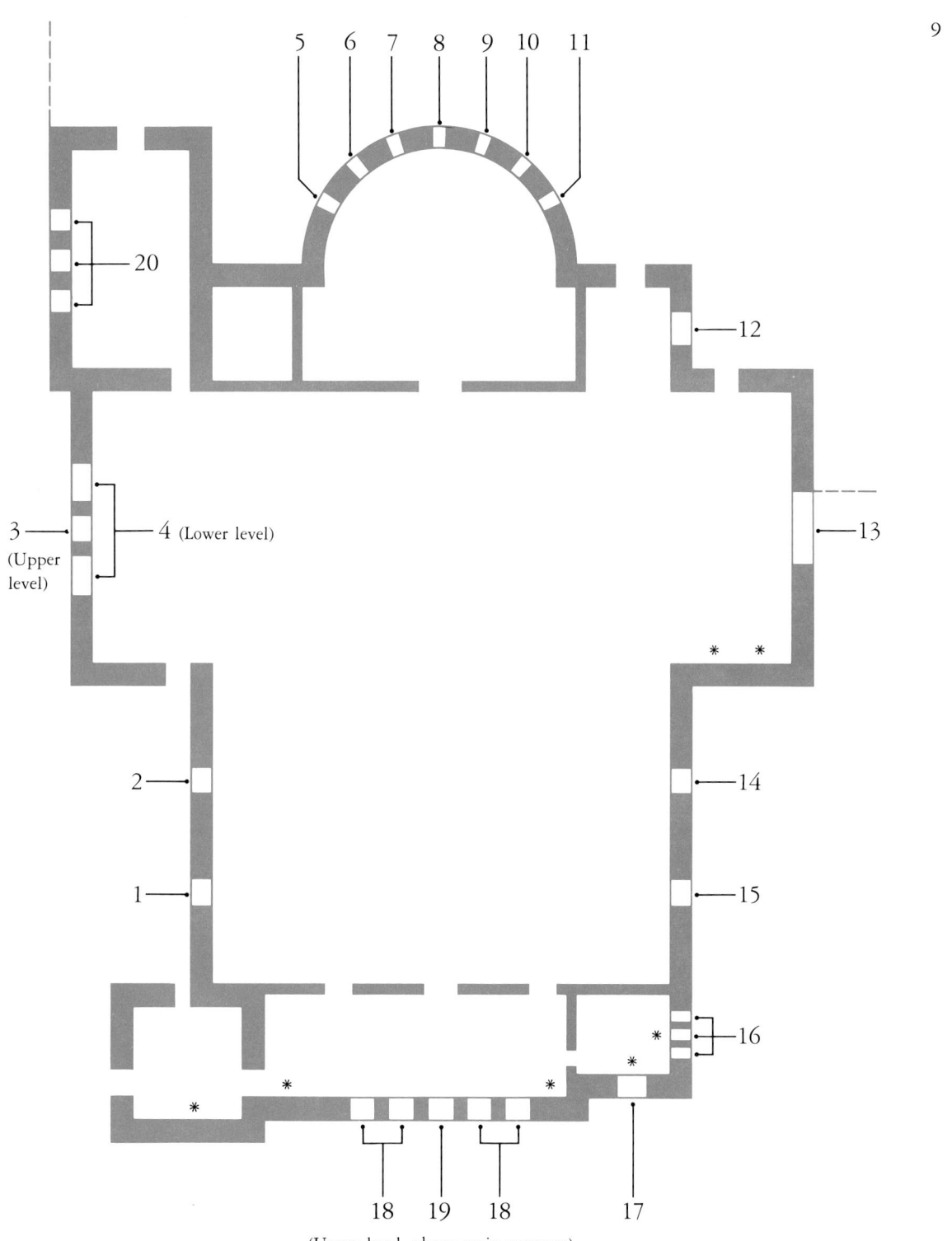

Brief History of the Church

EARLY HISTORY OF FIRST CHURCH

The roots of First Church in Cambridge, Congregational, can be traced back more than 350 years. During the early 1630s, thousands of Puritans fled England and the determination of Charles I to enforce conformity to the doctrine and rites of the Church of England. In 1632, a number of these Puritans gathered in Cambridge, then called Newtowne; they installed Thomas Hooker as their pastor a year later. In 1636, Hooker left for Hartford, Connecticut, taking all but eleven members of the congregation with him.

The Reverend Thomas Shepard was installed as pastor of the Newtowne congregation in 1636. His orthodox and inspirational preaching was a major factor in the selection of Newtowne as the site for a new college. Founded in 1636 with the specific purpose of educating ministers, the college was named after its first benefactor, John Harvard.

The congregation's early meetinghouses served as both places of worship and sites for town meetings. The first three structures, each with a distinctive bell tower, were undoubtedly town landmarks. The earliest meetinghouse was built by 1632 at the southwest corner of Dunster and Mount Auburn streets. About twenty years later, it was replaced by a second meetinghouse on Watch House Hill, located between the current Lehman Hall at Harvard and the subway kiosk. This building served the congregation for at least fifty years; a third place of worship was built on the same site by 1706.

After the building of the fourth meetinghouse in 1756, located just north of its predecessor, two significant events occurred. Several of "the richest and most aristocratic members" of the congregation, including Henry Vassall, Thomas Oliver, and Joseph Lee, wished to worship in accordance with Episcopalian beliefs. They left the church to establish a congregation of their own. Christ Church was built on Garden Street, just a few blocks from the fourth meetinghouse, in 1760, and it is still in use today.

A second division within the Congregational church body began to develop in 1829, this time between the Trinitarian and Unitarian factions. In 1833, the Unitarian group built, and its successors continue to use, the First Parish Church at the corner of Church Street and Massachusetts Avenue.

The Reverend Abiel Holmes retained the support of the Trinitarian faction, which made plans both for incorporation as the Shepard Congregational Society and for the building of a new church. The fifth meetinghouse, designed by Washington Allston in 1831, was located at the northwest corner of Holyoke and Mount Auburn streets, diagonally across the street from the congregation's earliest meetinghouse.

By the time Alexander McKenzie, the tenth minister of First Church, arrived in Cambridge in 1867, the small town had become a bustling metropolitan area with more than 40,000 inhabitants. Industrial opportunities in the town itself and public transportation to Boston made Cambridge a desirable place to live and worship.

McKenzie found the fifth meetinghouse to be "pleasant and convenient, although too small, after having been three times enlarged." The wooden building, an adaptation of the Greek Revival style, was a modest rectangular structure with an unadorned interior and clear-paned windows.

THE SIXTH MEETINGHOUSE

Land was purchased from Samuel Batchelder at the corner of Garden and Mason streets with the idea of creating a new and larger church in order to accommodate McKenzie's expanding congregation. The corner site was a prominent one, fronting on the Cambridge Common with the historic Washington elm located just a few feet away on Garden Street. Formerly the site of the Abraham Hill house built about 1718, the land had been vacant since the demolition of the house in 1863.

Abel C. Martin, an 1856 graduate of Harvard's Lawrence Scientific School, was chosen by the church's Building Committee to be the architect for the new structure. Alexander McKenzie and Martin were already acquainted, having both been members of Central Church on Winter Street in Boston. While it was rumored that McKenzie would have preferred his Harvard classmate, Henry Hobson Richardson, as architect, once Martin had been chosen by the Building Committee, the minister supported him wholeheartedly.

During his short lifetime of forty-four years (1835–1879), Martin designed a number of buildings, including residences, schools, hotels, and churches. He achieved particular recognition for his buildings' innovative ventilation systems, with First Church being a notable example.

Ground was broken for the Shepard Memorial Church on September 5, 1870, and the building was dedicated on May 22, 1872. The plan for the new structure contrasted dramatically with the earlier meetinghouses. Like a number of churches built after the Civil War in Cambridge, there was a move away from the traditional meetinghouse configuration to a much more elaborate structure.

Abel Martin, in describing his design for the Building Committee, stated that "the general character of the whole construction is determined by the use of the Round Arch." He goes on to say that "the English call it 'Norman,' but the true historic name is 'Romanesque,' which marks its descent from the old Roman Basilicas, the churches in which the early Christians first worshipped."

Both McKenzie and Martin had traveled in Europe during 1867 and were undoubtedly influenced by churches in England and on the Continent. An imposing structure, First Church was constructed of slate from a Medford quarry, with red granite trim and a dramatic 170-foot spire. Both the exterior and interior of the new church edifice were made more impressive by the use of many decorative details. McKenzie commented that "religion was intended to adorn the world, and we should not be satisfied with bare necessities."

The interior space, like the exterior, was a marked contrast to the previous, austere meetinghouses. Features such as the polygonal vaulted ceiling, the gilded dome in the apse, and the stenciled, terra-cotta-colored walls created a rich, ornate interior characteristic of many late nineteenth century structures. The pulpit occupied a prominent place in the cruciform plan, an idea favored by McKenzie and ideally suited to his eloquent preaching. In addition, there were galleries, located on the east and north side of the church, a feature reminiscent of the earlier meeting-houses. A *Cambridge Chronicle* article of the time described the church as "the largest, the most beautiful, and the most costly one in Cambridge," having been constructed for $135,000.

In 1873 a chapel was added behind the chancel, and the church's spire was completed. The chapel served a variety of uses: devotional services, Sunday School classes, and church meetings. A gilded cockerel weather vane that originally graced the spire of the New Brick or "Cockerel" Church on Hanover Street in Boston added a final touch. One of the oldest weather vanes made in New England and still in use, it was fabricated of copper by Deacon Shem Drowne in 1721.

ADDITIONS AND RENOVATIONS

There have been many additions and renovations since the church's completion in 1873. Some of the most significant changes occurred between 1924 and 1926. Raymond Calkins, the minister at the time, recalled why he felt the sanctuary needed renovation: "The general effect, with the terra-cotta colouring on the walls, was drab and dark. There were the makings of a beautiful church, but the beauty was not there." The architectural firm of Allen and Collens was chosen to renovate the sanctuary as well as to prepare plans for a new parish hall, office wing, and chapel.

Francis R. Allen and Charles Collens, both former students of the prestigious École des Beaux-Arts in Paris, were prominent architects in New York and Boston. The firm had a number of impressive clients and was recognized nationally for its design of churches, university buildings, and hospitals. Noteworthy examples of the firm's work prior to its association with First Church were: the Memorial Chapel at Union Theological Seminary in New York City, Andover Hall at the Harvard Divinity School in Cambridge, and the Leslie Lindsey Memorial Chapel at Emmanuel Church in Boston.

The remodeling of the sanctuary, inspired by early Roman basilicas as well as by Byzantine architecture, was completed in 1924. At this time, the gallery in the north transept was removed, making possible a full view of the large stained glass window on the north wall. In addition, ceiling rafters and purlins were added to give a greater impression of space.

The chancel changed dramatically. The entire area was enlarged to make room for the remodeled Hook and Hastings organ and seating for the choir. There was a greater expanse of wall space but with fewer windows; the number was reduced from nine to seven. Architect Charles Collens commented that "the chancel windows have been respaced and so located as to form a symmetrical treatment about the centre window, and have been decreased in number to admit the larger wall spaces consistent with the Romanesque style of architecture." The wooden communion table and pulpit were replaced by stone versions. A chancel railing of imported French stone was also added at that time.

The wall coloring before 1924 had been described in an 1892 article in the *Cambridge Tribune*. The writer referred to the "rich red coloring" of the walls and the "light sage green coloring of the ceiling." He commented that these colors harmonized with "the soft buff or salmon tint of the arches, while the reddish brown pillars stand out in fine relief with the bronzed capitals." As part of the 1924 renovations, the walls were painted the color of stone, creating a much more monochromatic background and a significantly different setting for the stained glass. The mysterious, dark sanctuary pierced with openings of multicolored glass was no longer. In its place was a much lighter interior with less contrast between the windows and their surroundings.

The renovation of the sanctuary was more expensive than anticipated; as a result, the

First Church with new 1938 steeple designed by Harold B. Willis. This view, taken from the intersection of Mason and Garden streets, shows the distinctive 1721 cockerel weather vane.

plans for the new office wing, parish hall, and chapel were not implemented. An alternative scheme was suggested by William H. McLean, a member of the congregation and an architect by training. In 1926, these additions were made using building materials and design motifs consistent with the original 1872 structure.

About ten years later, the church steeple was found to be structurally unsound. It was redesigned by Harold B. Willis, of Allen, Collens and Willis and rebuilt just before the 1938 hurricane. In the following year, the same architectural firm prepared plans for the interior of the chapel.

A bequest from Agnes Morton Lindsay in 1938 made possible the completion of the small chapel. The exterior of the chapel had been built as part of the 1926 addition, but the interior was left unfinished, with temporary walls, sparse furnishings, and no organ. In 1938, Architect Harold Willis commented on his design for the chapel: "we had in mind the architectural style and period already established in the church. This shows itself in the chapel in the round arches, a central European Romanesque of the eleventh or twelfth century. The simple barrel vaulted ceiling form is frequently met in this period, particularly in southern France. The altar was also designed in the same period. As Romanesque woodwork is generally of a heavy character, the chancel rail and pulpit have been designed in the transitory Gothic period frequently found in chapels in Europe."

Allen, Collens and Willis also designed the lighting fixtures, and the organ was built by the Estey Organ Company of Vermont. (It

First Church chancel, after the 1924 renovation by Allen and Collens, when the number of windows was reduced from nine to seven.

was later replaced with an Andover organ in 1958.) The chapel was consecrated on April 23, 1939, in memory of Edwin Parker Lindsay and Agnes Morton Lindsay.

In the sanctuary, the chancel was further modified in the 1970s. Both the organ and the choir were relocated once again, this time to the south transept. The Hook and Hastings organ was replaced with a Danish Frobenius organ, designed by Perry K. Neubauer, an architect and member of the congregation. He also designed an oak communion table with a large cross above it and a baptismal font. All were incorporated into the sanctuary in 1972, with the exception of the font, which was requested by Reverend Allen Happe and installed in 1979. As a result, the once separate parts of the church service, the sermon, communion, and baptism, were united and brought much closer to the congregation.

* * *

If Alexander McKenzie were to come back to his "cathedral" today, he would be reassured to see that the original church still stands, in fact, substantially enlarged. The cockerel still keeps watch from its lofty spire, and not only are the earliest stained glass windows still in place, but all the window openings are now filled with brightly colored pieces of glass.

Introduction to Stained Glass Windows

Glass is often stained or colored during its manufacture and, in some instances, details are added later to the surface. The terms "stained," "painted," or "stained and painted" are frequently used in describing glass. In this guide, all such windows will be referred to as "stained glass" windows.

The windows are identified by their subject matter or theme, with titles such as *St. Paul* or *The Good Shepherd*, or by the donors' names, such as the *Hart Window*. In the case of the *Fuller Window*, where neither the title nor the donor is known, the window is given the name of the family to whom it is dedicated.

The stained glass was installed in existing window openings over a period of eighty-nine years, from 1872 to 1960. Of the nineteen large windows in the sanctuary, at least eleven, and probably thirteen, were installed during the forty-five years between 1867 to 1912, when Alexander McKenzie was minister. Of the remaining windows, one was installed during Raymond Calkins's ministry, four during John Leamon's tenure, and one was begun under Calkins and completed forty-two years later when John Leamon was minister. In addition, there are seven small lunettes about which little is known in the sanctuary, and a group of windows in the chapel.

WINDOW STYLES

Four styles of stained glass are represented in First Church, reflecting nine decades of stained glass design. The *Horsford Rose Window* of 1872 is the earliest window and sole example of late nineteenth century English stained glass. The ten subsequent window installations from 1894 to 1908 represent the opalescent style; eight of these are documented Tiffany windows. The *Kimball/Rice Window* of 1918 represents a break with the opalescent style and is more in the European tradition. It was followed in 1929 by the *Bancroft Window*, the first of five windows in the Gothic Revival style.

THE HORSFORD ROSE WINDOW

In the 1870s, many churches in the United States imported stained glass windows from England, France, and Germany. A wide variety of styles was represented because of stylistic differences not only within countries but also within individual studios. At that time, most of the previously lost technical achievements of the Gothic age were retrieved, and there was a reinterpretation of medieval glass combined with both Renaissance and nineteenth century ideas.

The *Horsford Rose Window* of 1872 is the only imported window in First Church. It was "made of English glass by celebrated London artists," according to church records

Detail of Horsford Rose Window (p. 25)

and newspaper articles of the time. Unfortunately, no reference is ever made to a specific London studio. There are stylistic similarities with other stained glass windows by London studios of that period, such as Clayton & Bell and Heaton, Butler & Bayne, but the Horsford window's provenance remains unknown.

The window draws inspiration from both the medieval and Renaissance past, but stylistically, it belongs to the late nineteenth century. The figures, with their richly embroidered robes, are highly decorative and brilliantly colored. The images are created through the use of colored paints fused to single pieces of glass. The leading frames each section, in contrast with medieval windows, which contain many small glass pieces held in place by leading.

THE OPALESCENT ERA

The appearance of the next window, *The Good Shepherd*, in 1894 marked the arrival of the opalescent era at First Church. Opalescent glass, manufactured in the United States, had become the latest fashion. Dissatisfied with imported stained glass of inferior quality, Louis Comfort Tiffany and John LaFarge developed opalescent glass in the 1870s. This uniquely American form of glass, translucent but not transparent, was fashioned into a variety of textures and colors. While a number of other artists, such as the Lamb brothers, Maitland Armstrong, and Henry Crowninshield, worked with the new kind of glass, it was Tiffany who capitalized on the technique. The name "Tiffany" was to become virtually synonymous with opalescent glass.

The opalescent window designs are a result of the combination of color variations within the glass itself and a layering

Detail of opalescent window Angel (p. 32)

technique. Shapes are created through leading rather than through an extensive use of enameling. The Tiffany firm applied minimal enamel details, usually restricted to facial areas, hands, and lettering. The enameling was applied to either the back or front of the glass. Unfortunately, in some instances the paint did not always vitrify or harden, and peeling occurred in later years.

In some opalescent windows, as many as six layers of glass were used. Unfortunately, with the passage of time, the multiple layers permitted the intrusion of dirt and grime as well as severe buckling.

There are twelve opalescent windows at First Church, ten of which were installed during the fifteen-year period from 1894 to 1908. At least eight are known to have been created by the Tiffany firm, although none are signed. The origin of the other four opalescent windows is unclear.

While for the majority of the Tiffany windows the designer is not known, in two instances a particular artist is given credit. W. Frederick Wilson is cited as the designer for *The Four Elements* and Joseph Lauber for the *Resurrection Angel*. Wilson was considered one of the foremost designers in Tiffany's firm and was responsible for several windows at the 1893 Columbian Exposition in Chicago. Joseph Lauber had his own studio until he joined the Tiffany firm in the 1890s. He designed not only stained glass windows but also altars, predella, and sedilia.

THE KIMBALL/RICE WINDOW

In 1918, ten years after the last Tiffany window was installed, the *Kimball/Rice Window* was designed by the Horace J. Phipps studio. Only the center portion and the three tracery windows were executed and installed at that time. Forty-two years later, a contribution from Mr. and Mrs. Frederick A. Rice assured the completion of the side panels by the Willet Studios of Philadelphia, using the original Phipps design. The largest single window in First Church, the *Kimball/Rice Window* marks a departure from the opalescent style. Three-dimensional images are created through an extensive use of painting, with the result being closer to the European stained glass traditions. Religious figures and their appropriate symbols are set in an elaborate architectural framework. The occasional intrusion of leads is a subtle reminder that this is a stained glass window, not a painting.

THE GOTHIC REVIVAL ERA

The five most recent windows, installed between 1929 and 1957, look to the earliest years of stained glass, the medieval period, for their inspiration. With the installation of the *Bancroft Window* in 1929, the Gothic Revival era commenced for First Church. The window bears the name of the firm that created it, the Reynolds, Francis and Rohnstock studio of Boston. The four most recent windows, *Mary of Bethany*, *Dorcas*, *Christ Blessing Little Children*, and the *Lester Grisaille Windows*, all installed in 1957, are the work of the Willet Studios of Philadelphia.

By 1929, stained glass artists in the United States had become fascinated with Gothic churches and medieval glass. Many books were written by laypeople, architects, and stained glass artists about the special qualities of medieval glass in cathedrals such as Chartres in France. *Mont Saint Michel and Chartres* by Henry Adams and *Adventures in Light and Color* by Charles Connick are two notable examples. Stained glass artists like Connick, Reynolds, and Willet traveled to Europe to study medieval glass and were greatly influenced by what they saw. Architects and stained glass artists alike enthusiastically recommended Gothic Revival glass, though often with little regard for the architectural style of the building.

Detail of Kimball/Rice Window (p. 39)

The *Bancroft Window* of 1929 and the Lester windows of 1957 show the Gothic Revival era's fondness for medieval techniques in the background use of grisaille glass. A twelfth century innovation, grisaille glass is characterized by a geometric pattern with painted, stylized foliage. The word "grisaille" is derived from the French word "gris," meaning "grey," because of the dark paints commonly used in this technique. The decorative glass, less expensive to make than the more ornate pictorial windows, has been a popular stained glass style since its introduction some 800 years ago.

The *Bancroft Window's* painted details, irregular leading pattern, primary colors, and grisaille background all evoke the twelfth and thirteenth centuries. The three-dimensional angel, however, reflects the influence of Renaissance ideas and is a decided contrast with two-dimensional medieval figures.

In 1957, twenty-eight years after the *Bancroft Window* was installed, the last four groups of windows were added. Two windows in the apse, *Dorcas* and *Mary of Bethany*, a group of four grisaille windows, and an oculus window in the balcony were designed in the Gothic Revival style by artists from the Willet Studios of Philadelphia.

Dorcas and *Mary of Bethany* were designed by Marguerite Gaudin of the Willet Studios. The windows, with their small pieces of brightly colored glass, patchwork of leading, and extensive use of paint, convey a medieval feeling. But like the *Bancroft Window*, the modeling and three-dimensional look of the figures place the windows squarely in the twentieth century.

The oculus window, *Christ Blessing Little Children,* and the *Lester Grisaille Windows*

Center lancet of Bancroft Window (p. 42)

are again creations of the Willet Studios. Designed by John Kevorkian, both windows were donated by Mrs. Horace Hardy Lester.

DECISION MAKERS

Many people contributed to the decision making process at First Church: donors, stained glass artists, ministers, bequest committees, and church architects. There was no single, consistent approach, in contrast with other churches where guidelines were set down by an architect or church officials.

Among the decisions required for each window were choice of studio, window location, subject matter, and type of glass. Often a number of stained glass studios were considered before the donor or bequest committee made a choice. The Wednesday Informal Group and Mrs. Lester, for example, donors of two different windows, contacted the Willet and Reynolds studios, among others. The Kimball/Rice committee looked at windows in different churches and also consulted a number of studios before deciding on the Phipps firm.

Window locations were chosen by a variety of interested people. A minister, Alexander McKenzie, suggested the center chancel window over the altar as an appropriate location for *The Good Shepherd*. The Kimball/Rice Bequest Committee asked the Phipps studio to execute drawings for two window locations, the center balcony and the north transept, before deciding on the latter. In another instance, Charles Theodore Russell in an 1897 letter states that he believed his family had "the right" to install a window across from *St. Paul*, which was earlier donated by his mother.

It was not unusual for donors to recommend a particular kind of glass for their windows. The *Horsford Rose Window* was created from English "cathedral" glass, and the Horsford family recommended that type of glass for future church windows. However, twenty-three years later the family chose fashionable Tiffany opalescent glass for *The Four Elements*, and subsequent Horsford windows were commissioned from the Tiffany Studios.

The Kimball/Rice committee submitted a resolution at the annual meeting in 1918 whereby the parish was to approve all future stained glass. The following resolution was ratified: "All stained glass memorial shall be of such type of glass as may be established for the church, and must be designed and executed by such stained glass manufacturers as shall be approved by the Parish. All stained glass windows shall follow in subject matter and general design any program which may be adapted by the Parish." It is unclear whether or not the Parish did in fact approve subsequent stained glass windows. In 1960, for example, Mrs. Lester sent her own guidelines to the Willet Studios, specifying not only the kind of glass but also how it was to be installed, as well as a number of other technical details.

STAINED GLASS SUBJECTS

Choosing an appropriate subject for each window often involved a number of individuals, including, at times, the donor, the stained glass studio, and the church architects. Church records give some indication as to how and why the subject matter was chosen for a number of windows.

Donors often made suggestions about the subject matter. For the *Horsford Rose Window*, the Horsford family chose the subject of Mary and suggested that family crests and other motifs be incorporated into the design. The donors of both *The Good Shepherd* and *Faith* chose the subjects. Mrs. Lester conducted extensive research on stained glass and consulted at length with the Willet Studios before submitting a design for her grisaille windows.

In other instances, the stained glass studio or the church architects influenced the choice of subject. W. Frederick Wilson of the Tiffany Studios chose the subject for *The Four Elements*. E. Crosby Willet of the Willet Studios proposed the subjects of Dorcas and Mary of Bethany to the Wednesday Informal Group. The church architects, Allen and Collens, advised Jacob Bancroft on an appropriate subject for his grisaille window.

The majority of First Church windows have some religious or biblical association. New Testament figures include Paul, Dorcas, Mary of Bethany, John the Baptist, and John the Evangelist. Other figures, such as angels, are found in both the Old and New Testaments. Interestingly, one window depicts Catherine of Alexandria, a historic figure who was considered a saint by the Roman Catholic church but was recently de-canonized because of new historical evidence. Examples that do not have a specific religious reference are the ornamental opalescent, grisaille, and *Fuller* windows.

Angels are the most common window theme, appearing in eight of the nineteen windows. Indeed, angels play an important role in Old and New Testament stories, often as heavenly messengers between God and people, protecting the righteous and punishing wrongdoers. The angel theme was a popular one in late nineteenth century church windows in the United States; First Church was no exception.

While varying in shape and size, the angels all figure prominently in the window designs. A single angel dominates the *Bancroft*, *Angel*, and *Resurrection Angel* windows. Both angels and human forms are seen in the *They Shall Be Mine, Saith the Lord*, *Hart*, *Horsford Rose*, and *Kimball/Rice* windows. *The Four Elements* seem to have an infinite number of angels; in fact, there are thirty-one. Some of the figures are purely decorative, like the angels in the *Horsford Rose Window* and the *Angel* window. The smaller angels in the *Kimball/Rice* and *The Four Elements* windows also fulfill that role. In other instances, the angels are more symbolic. The four large angels in *The Four Elements* represent air, fire, earth, and water. In the *Resurrection Angel*, the figure embodies the title. In the *Kimball/Rice Window*, the Angel of the Annunciation is depicted in the center section. In the *Hart Window* and *They Shall Be Mine, Saith the Lord*, the angels play a more protective role.

Women have a similarly important thematic position, appearing in twelve windows. In *Mary of Bethany*, *Faith*, *St. Catherine of Alexandria*, and *Dorcas*, a woman is the central figure. In the *Kimball/Rice Window*, Mary is the focus of the center panel. A woman and child are depicted in the *Fuller Window*, while Christ and Mary are the focus of the *Horsford Rose Window*. Women figures appear in the background of *Christ Blessing Little Children*. Angels are often depicted as females, as in *The Four Elements*, *Angel*, *They Shall Be Mine, Saith the Lord*, and the *Hart Window*.

DONORS AND DEDICATIONS

Most of First Church's windows are dedicated to one or more members of a family; children, parents, and sisters are memorialized. In the *St. Catherine of Alexandria*, *Hart*, and *Fuller* windows, a child is honored. The *Horsford Rose Window* was given in memory of a sister. *St. Paul* was given by Mrs. Russell in honor of her husband, and later, *Faith* was given by the Russell sons in memory of their mother. Jacob Bancroft gave the grisaille window in memory of both his parents and sister. Interestingly, each of the Lester windows bears both an individual family dedication, such as to Mrs. Lester's parents, and a collective dedication, such as "To All Mothers and Fathers."

With only four exceptions, First Church's windows are dedicated to women. The four exceptions are those dedicated to Charles Russell, Horace Putnam Hart, and Alexander McKenzie (two windows).

In addition to families, donors of stained glass included church organizations and friends. Women's organizations such as the Shepard Guild, the Nevertheless Circle of King's Daughters, and the Wednesday Informal Group commissioned windows. The Shepard Guild honored young women, while the Wednesday Informal Group paid tribute to a member of their own organization, Elizabeth Emma Morrill. The Nevertheless Circle and friends of Alexander McKenzie each gave a window in his honor.

*   *   *

The stained glass of First Church represents a number of different styles from the nineteenth and twentieth centuries. While lacking stylistic unity, the windows reflect a certain harmony that is created through repetition of subjects, motifs, and shapes.

Repeated themes provide links between many windows. Paul, for example, is seen in *St. Catherine of Alexandria*, where he appears as a statue, and in *St. Paul*, where he is the main figure. The mother and child theme appears in both the *Fuller Window* and the center panel of the *Kimball/Rice Window*. Mary of Bethany is represented in both the *Horsford Rose Window* and the window named after her. As mentioned earlier, angels play a major visual role, appearing in eight windows.

Several recurring motifs can also be seen. For example, a lamb is present in both *The Good Shepherd* and the *Kimball/Rice Window*. A crown is the focal point of *They Shall Be Mine, Saith the Lord* and is part of the upper section of the *Fuller Window*. Lilies are a feature of the *Resurrection Angel*, *Hart*, and *Kimball/Rice* windows.

The window shapes themselves create a rhythmic harmony, united by their curved configuration. In addition, other design features, such as window borders and architectural framework, lend a sense of continuity.

The following chronological guide details the history and design of each of the nineteen windows in the sanctuary. It is intended to give the viewer a greater understanding and appreciation of the stained glass at First Church.

Guide to the Windows

To provide historical perspective, the windows in this guide are discussed in chronological order.

The windows are numbered according to location on the Window Diagram, page 9.

Detail of The Four Elements (p. 29)

[3] Horsford Rose Window

DATE: 1872
STUDIO: unknown
DEDICATION: Mary L'Hommedieu Gardiner Horsford
DONOR: Phoebe Gardiner Horsford

The *Horsford Rose Window*, the oldest example of stained glass at First Church, is just one instance of the Horsford family's generosity. Throughout the nineteenth and twentieth centuries, no family contributed more to the church's beautification than the Horsfords. Two other stained glass windows, as well as a number of decorative additions, such as lighting fixtures, a lectern, a communion table cross, and communion ware, are other examples of their munificence.

Early references to the rose window in newspaper articles and church records state that it was "made of English glass by celebrated London artists," with no mention made of a specific design studio. A Building Committee report declared the window "admirable in design and good taste." The committee commented that the kind of glass, "cathedral," was the same as that used in the early churches in England.

A memorial booklet offers a clue about the subject matter of the window. Mary is depicted at Christ's feet in the window's center section and is surrounded by eight roundels with alternating seraphim and cherubim. The words "Mary sat at Jesus' feet and heard his words" (Luke 10:39) are incorporated into the center panel of the window. Mary Horsford's love of flowers is illustrated by a rose of Sharon and a lily of the valley in the center portion of the window.

Unlike any other windows in First Church, there are numerous genealogical references. Family coats of arms represented are those of the Sylvester family, in the uppermost section, the Horsford family, on the right, and the Gardiner family, on the left. In the lower center circle, an angel bears a scroll reading "L'Hommedieu, Eid Genossen," the Gardiner family motto.

Mary Horsford, the first wife of Eben Norton Horsford, died at age thirty-one, shortly after the birth of her fourth daughter. She was a poet and author of "Indian Legends and Other Poems." According to family records, one of her favorite quotations was "When the Chief Shepherd shall appear, Ye shall receive a crown of glory" (I Peter 5:4). The words are incorporated into the window given in her memory.

Mary Horsford wrote the following poem with one of her children in mind.

"I cannot in the future look,
　The augury to prove;
But earthly joys and earthly woes
　Must human spirits move;
And she, like all, must strive with care,
Disasters meet, and suffering bear.

But I will teach her hopefully
　To meet what Fate betides;
To live and labor earnestly,
　In narrow path or wide;
And, with salt tears on paling cheek,
　A benediction still to speak."

26

[8] The Good Shepherd

DATE: 1894
STUDIO: The Tiffany Glass & Decorating Company
DEDICATION: Dedicated to the work of young women in the Church
DONOR: The Shepard Guild

The earliest Tiffany window in First Church, *The Good Shepherd*, has always occupied a prominent position in the center of the chancel wall. The Shepard Guild, founded in 1892, donated the window.

Named in honor of Reverend Thomas Shepard's first wife, Margaret Shepard, the Guild was composed of young women in the church. Alexander McKenzie encouraged the formation of the women's group, which focused on missionary support, at home and abroad, as well as church beautification. The minister suggested the idea of contributing a stained glass window to be placed above the communion table.

The Guild members chose both the stained glass studio, The Tiffany Glass & Decorating Company, and the subject for the window. The Good Shepherd theme was one of the most popular during the nineteenth century. It was not unusual for stained glass designers or their clients to look to oil paintings for inspiration in portraying this figure. The First Church window design is closely patterned after a painting of "The Good Shepherd" by Bernhard Plockhorst (1825–1907), a popular German artist.

The Guild raised money by sponsoring a number of events, such as the "Maids of Greece," which was held in Brattle Hall. According to a member of the Guild, "the window was first shown in the small Tiffany Chapel at the World's Fair in Chicago" in 1893. As a result, the Tiffany studio made a concession in price for the First Church window.

The Tiffany firm used a relatively small amount of enamel on the glass. Some of the paint has deteriorated over time, primarily in the flesh areas, the lamb, and the inscription. The original words appear to read, "presented by the Shepard Guild as a memorial to the work of the young women of this church."

28

[4] The Four Elements

DATE: 1895
STUDIO: The Tiffany Glass & Decorating Company
DEDICATION: Phoebe Gardiner Horsford and Eben Norton Horsford
DONOR: Bequest of Eben Norton Horsford

W. Frederick Wilson, a British stained glass artist with the Tiffany studio, designed *The Four Elements*. A newspaper article of the time notes that the subject was chosen by Wilson and that "over one hundred thousand separate pieces of glass and one half ton of lead and solder was used to hold pieces in position." The article continues by saying, "it has taken a year to complete the windows which it is said, cost several thousand dollars."

The Four Elements is the first of three Tiffany windows to be installed in 1895. The two lancets, placed within a stone framework, comprise the largest set of windows in the church. The robes of the four large angels, fashioned out of drapery glass, are an excellent example of the kind of glass for which Tiffany was famous.

The elements of earth, air, fire, and water are represented by four large angels. The theme is an appropriate one for Professor Horsford, who was Harvard's Rumford Professor of Natural Sciences. The idea of the four elements had been incorporated into Christian thought from Greek philosophy: fire and air represent the ethereal; earth, solidity; and water, a transitional force.

It was not unusual for Tiffany designs to be used more than one time, although the studio did not publicize this fact. The four principal angels in the Horsford window are also present in a window entitled "Gloria in Excelsis" in the Second Reformed Church in Hackensack, New Jersey. There are significant differences between the two sets of windows. The shapes of the windows are not similar, and the order of the four large angels differs. In addition, the New Jersey window has neither the smaller angels nor an inscription. The date of the "Gloria" window is undetermined, but it is known to have been installed in 1909. According to church records, the New Jersey stained glass was part of the Tiffany exhibition at the Chicago World's Fair in 1893.

The Four Elements contains a number of inscriptions. The banner carried by the four angels reads: "O, ye Mountains and Hills and all green Things, bless ye the Lord. O, ye Showers and Dews, bless ye the Lord. O, ye Seas and Floods, bless ye the Lord. O, ye Fire and Heat, bless ye the Lord" (Inspiration of Psalm 148). There are additional inscriptions displayed on the banner intertwined with the smaller angels that read: "Praise ye Him, all His angels, Praise ye Him all His Hosts, O praise thee Lord, ye Angel of His. Ye that . . . fulfill his Commands." Within the quatrefoil shapes at the top of the windows, the inscription reads, "The smoke of the incense [with the] prayers of the saints ascended up before God" (Revelation 8:4).

The Four Elements incorporates the name of Eben Norton Horsford and his second wife, Phoebe Gardiner Horsford, who died five years after the window was installed.

[2] They Shall Be Mine, Saith the Lord

DATE: 1895
STUDIO: The Tiffany Glass & Decorating Company
DEDICATION: Mary Horsford Curtis
DONOR: Phoebe Gardiner Horsford

Phoebe Gardiner Horsford donated the earliest window at First Church in memory of her sister and this second window in memory of her sister's daughter, Mary Horsford Curtis. While a British firm was chosen for the *Horsford Rose Window,* twenty-three years later Phoebe Horsford commissioned the prestigious Tiffany studio to design this window.

A crown is depicted in both the Curtis window (as the main focal point) and the *Fuller Window* (in its upper section). While in many Tiffany windows jewel-like glass prisms are incorporated into crowns, at First Church a similar effect is achieved through enameling on glass. In addition to the crown, there are other symbols, such as the processional cross and mirror with the flaming heart, representing religious fervor.

An inscription reads, "They shall be mine, saith the Lord of Hosts, in that day when I make up my jewels" (Malachi 3:17). Mary Horsford Curtis died in 1893 at the age of thirty-eight years.

[7] Fuller Window

DATE: 1895
STUDIO: unknown
DEDICATION: Harriet Maria Fuller and her son, Charles Richard Fuller
DONOR: unknown

In 1895, the church calendar noted that "a new window" in the chancel "was installed in memory of Mrs. Charles L. Fuller and her son, Charles Richard Fuller." Unfortunately, no mention was made of the donor or the stained glass studio responsible for the design. It is likely the window was donated by Charles L. Fuller in memory of his wife, who died the previous year, and their son, who died seven years earlier.

The mother and child theme is a familiar one in the art world and especially in nineteenth century stained glass. Here, the child is a young boy, possibly the same age as Charles Richard Fuller, who died at the age of twelve.

There are similarities between the *Fuller Window* and the two opalescent chancel windows, *Angel* and *The Good Shepherd*. Each has two to three layers of glass, textural details achieved through enameling, a setting with a suggestion of columns, and an inscription. While the other two are Tiffany windows, the provenance of the *Fuller Window* remains a mystery.

The inscription reads, "In memoriam, Harriet Maria Fuller 1843–1894. Charles Richard Fuller 1875–1888." The probable donor, Harriet's husband, Charles L. Fuller, died a year after the window was installed.

[9] Angel

DATE: 1895
STUDIO: The Tiffany Glass & Decorating Company
DEDICATION: Alexander McKenzie
DONOR: The Nevertheless Circle of King's Daughters

The first of two windows dedicated to the Reverend Alexander McKenzie, *Angel* was given by the Nevertheless Circle of King's Daughters in 1895. The women's group was one of many dedicated to helping "those less fortunate" in the late nineteenth century. Dr. McKenzie encouraged the formation of organizations with names such as Steadfast Circle, Holdfast Circle, and Loving Service Circle. These groups at First Church were relatively small, each having approximately twenty-five women members.

The *Angel* window, like the two earlier chancel examples, *The Good Shepherd* and the *Fuller Window*, is divided into three parts. There is a cross in the upper section, a single angel in the center, and a panel with an inscription at the base. The cross contains the letters, IHN. The letters IH are the first initials of Jesus's name in Greek, and the letter N stands for Nike, meaning victor.

The inscription for the window includes the motto for the women's group, "Nevertheless, not my will but thine be done" (Luke 22:42). An earlier part of the inscription reads, "The Nevertheless Circle of King's Daughters place this window in commemoration of the many years of loving service given to this Church of Christ by Reverend Alexander McKenzie DD."

〖14〗 Resurrection Angel

DATE: 1897
STUDIO: The Tiffany Glass & Decorating Company
DEDICATION: Alexander McKenzie's Thirty Years of Service to First Church
DONOR: Friends of Alexander McKenzie

Two of the most popular Tiffany window themes were the Resurrection Angel and the Good Shepherd. There are at least seventy Tiffany examples of each subject in the United States today.

Resurrection Angel is one of the two Tiffany windows at First Church whose designer is known; it was designed by Joseph Lauber. An earlier window, *The Four Elements,* was designed by W. Frederick Wilson in 1895.

Resurrection Angel was presented to Alexander McKenzie by a group of friends on January 24, 1897. The minister's response was noted in a commemorative booklet. He remarked that "the angel stands with feet upon the ground, but with face turned towards the light from above. Thus should the minister stand." He continues by saying that the minister is "with his people that he might give all the light to them, all the grace and truth which God gave to him for them."

[15] St. Paul

DATE: 1898
STUDIO: The Tiffany Glass & Decorating Company
DEDICATION: Charles Theodore Russell
DONOR: Sarah Elizabeth Russell

Charles Theodore Russell, long affiliated with First Church, was a prominent member of the Boston legal community. In addition to founding a law firm with his brother, T.S. Russell, in 1845, he was a professor at Boston University Law School and the author of a book entitled *Manhood Suffrage*.

Reverend McKenzie and Russell were acquaintances since the 1850s, when they were both members of Central Church in Boston. By 1855, the Russell family had moved to Cambridge and subsequently joined First Church.

St. Paul and *Faith,* another window given by the Russell family, both feature statuelike figures. In earlier chancel windows, there is a suggestion of an architectural framework, a column or colonnade at the corners. In both Russell windows, the setting is more clearly defined, and the figures are depicted within an elaborate Renaissance niche.

The Apostle Paul is frequently represented in stained glass windows as a bald-headed figure with a book of his epistles and a sword representing his martyrdom. Here there is no reminder of his death; rather, the emphasis is on his oratorial and scholarly qualities. Included in the window design is the inscription, "Now I Paul myself beseech you by the meekness and gentleness of Christ" (2 Corinthians 10:1).

[1] Faith

DATE: 1898
STUDIO: The Tiffany Glass & Decorating Company
DEDICATION: Sarah Elizabeth Russell
DONOR: Russell sons: Charles, Joseph, and Henry

While the Tiffany studios were completing the *St. Paul* window in honor of Charles Theodore Russell, the donor, Mrs. Russell, died. Shortly thereafter, the Russell sons contacted the Tiffany studio and commissioned a window in memory of their mother. In a letter to George S. Saunders, a church official, Charles Theodore Russell, Jr. wrote that he assumes "we have a right to occupy" the window opening across the sanctuary from *St. Paul.* He suggested creating a window that would harmonize with that of Paul.

There are a number of similarities between the two Russell windows. Each portrays a single figure set in a niche, with an inscription in the lower panel. Both figures are richly robed and each holds a book; in addition, the two windows contain many of the same colors.

There are also a number of differences between the two windows. One depicts a real figure, Paul, and the other an allegorical figure, Faith. Paul faces the viewer, addressing his audience with an outstretched hand and an open book. Faith looks away from the audience, toward the heavens, clasping a closed book to her breast.

The inscription in the lower panel of the window reads, "When I call to Remembrance the unfeigned Faith that is in thee. In memory of Sarah Elizabeth Russell" (2 Timothy 1:5).

[12] Hart Window

DATE: 1901
STUDIO: unknown
DEDICATION: Horace Putnam Hart
DONOR: Professor and Mrs. Albert Bushnell Hart

At one time, this memorial window occupied a prominent place over the baptistry font. However, an addition to the church in 1924 prevents natural light from coming through the glass. With the current baptismal font located in the center of the chancel, the *Hart Window* is rarely seen. It is visible only when artificially lit from behind. (The wall switch is opposite the window.)

The window was given by Professor and Mrs. Hart in memory of a child who died at birth. The couple later adopted twin sons, Adrian and Albert, Jr. Professor Albert Bushnell Hart was a renowned historian and professor of history at Harvard for nearly fifty years. An authority on international affairs as well as on George Washington, "Bushy," distinguished by his very long, white beard, was a familiar sight on campus.

It is not known which American glass studio designed the window. Like many opalescent windows, there are multiple layers of glass. In 1987, the window was removed because of severe buckling and was restored. At that time, it was discovered that there were at least two layers of glass throughout, and in some places, three layers.

As in an earlier window, *Resurrection Angel,* an angel is depicted in a setting of white lilies. Here the angel takes on a protective role as she cradles a small baby in her arms. The inscription reads, "For where your treasure is, there will your heart be also" (Luke 12:34).

[19] St. Catherine of Alexandria

DATE: 1908
STUDIO: Tiffany Studios
DEDICATION: Martha Theresa Fiske
DONOR: Mr. and Mrs. Josiah M. Fiske

One of the most popular themes in Renaissance painting was St. Catherine of Alexandria. Often portrayed with a spiked wheel, a symbol of her martyrdom, Catherine represented saintliness, beauty, and learning. At First Church, Catherine is portrayed as a young woman in a garden setting with a statue of Paul. The focus is on her scholarly nature, and there is little reminder of her grisly death. In the background is an Egyptian bas-relief depicting, among other figures, Osiris and his mother or sister.

The last Tiffany window to be installed in First Church is given in memory of a young woman, Martha Theresa Fiske. The scholar theme is an appropriate one for Miss Fiske, who was an accomplished academician, teacher, and author when she died in 1907 at the age of thirty. She was one of the early presidents of the Shepard Guild and author of a book entitled *The World and the Word*. Dedicated to missionary efforts, her Bible contained the words, "When my Heavenly Father calls me from this world to higher service there is just one word that I should like to have remembered in connection with my name, and this is 'Missions,' the cause for which my savior lived and died."

It is a combination of elements—the setting, the figure of Catherine, and the stonework—that make the window one of the most interesting and appealing in First Church.

38

〖13〗 Kimball/Rice Window

DATE: 1918/1960
STUDIO: Design by Horace J. Phipps and Company

1918: Center lancet and three tracery windows by Horace J. Phipps and Company
DEDICATION: Harriet T. Neally Kimball
DONOR: Bequest of W. Frederick Kimball

1960: Two side lancets completed according to Phipps design by The Willet Stained Glass Studios, Inc.
DEDICATION: "To the Glory of God and the Service of His Church"
DONOR: Mr. and Mrs. Frederick A. Rice

An unexpected bequest of $2,000 was received from the estate of W. Frederick Kimball in 1917. The bequest specified that a window was to be commissioned in honor of Kimball's wife, Harriet T. Neally Kimball, a former public school teacher.

A committee was appointed to choose an appropriate stained glass studio. Architect Charles Collens and a representative of the donor were among those on the committee. After viewing windows in other local churches, including Trinity Church in Boston, the firm of Horace J. Phipps and Company was selected. Charles Collens requested drawings and estimates for two window locations, one over the east gallery and the other over the gallery in the north transept. In January 1918, there was a unanimous decision to place the window in the north transept. While the studio submitted a design for the entire window, only the center lancet and three traceries above were executed and installed in 1918.

The *Kimball/Rice Window* is the largest and most complex in First Church. Like *The Four Elements,* it is set into a stone framework, in contrast with the wooden frames of other windows. Its style is closer to European stained glass traditions and is a marked contrast with the earlier opalescent windows. The center lancet depicts the Mother and Child, the Annunciation scene with two angels, and there is an inscription in the lower section. Incorporated into the lancet are the words "In the beginning was the word and the word was God" (John 1:1). The inscription in the lower panel reads, "In loving memory of Harriet T. Neally Kimball (1852–1904) by her husband, W. Frederick Kimball (1852–1916)." In the three tracery windows above are the words "There shall be no end to his kingdom" (Luke 1:33).

An elaborate architectural framework creates the setting for the figures and symbols in the window. A church manual of 1920 noted that the main color scheme of the Phipps window was "ruby, blue and gold" and that "the ornaments correspond with the architecture of the building."

In December 1958, Mr. and Mrs. Frederick A. Rice requested that the Willet Studios of Philadelphia complete the two side panels from the original Phipps design. Mrs. Rice died unexpectedly in 1959, but the stained glass studio carried out the windows as planned. A memorandum from the Willet Studios to First Church suggests the difficulty of the project: "The creation of these panels, a feat far more difficult than making an entirely new window, was carried through, under the personal supervision of Dr. Willet, by Raymond DeHaven, an artist of the greatest skill and long standing with the Willet Studios."

The left panel depicts John the Baptist, a figure who appeared frequently in stained glass windows, particularly in medieval English glass. In the upper part of the lancet, John, dressed in animal skins and a cloak, is seen with his usual symbol, a staff with a cross at the top. In addition, he has a water flask at his waist, symbolizing his wilderness stay. He carries a scroll that reads, "Ecce Agnus Dei" (Behold the Lamb of God). Both the scroll and the small medallion at the top of the panel allude to his prophecy as the forerunner of Christ. Jesus is symbolized by the lamb bearing a banner of victory on the book of seals. The lower scene depicts the Baptism of Christ in the River Jordan. The medallion above contains a baptismal symbol, a font flanked by scallop shells, and the dove of the Holy Spirit.

St. John the Evangelist is depicted in the right panel. In the upper section of the lancet, he is shown writing his Gospel, and his symbol, an eagle, is shown above him. In the lower part of the panel, John is shown as an old man on the island of Patmos with the book of Revelations on his lap. There is a vision of Christ seated on a rainbow, holding seven stars in his hand with seven candlesticks (Revelation 1:12–16). The double-edged sword of the spirit is coming from his mouth. A medallion above the scene depicts a chalice with a serpent emerging from it, alluding to the legend that St. John's enemies tried to murder him by poisoning the Communion wine.

Detail of center tracery stained glass, Kimball/Rice Window, installed in 1918

Left: Detail of center lancet, below Annunciation scene, Kimball/Rice Window

⟦16⟧ Bancroft Window

DATE: 1929
STUDIO: Reynolds, Francis and Rohnstock
DEDICATION: Joseph, Maria, and Martha Bancroft
DONOR: Jacob Bancroft

Jacob Bancroft was a lawyer by profession and a "quiet, humble man," according to Reverend Raymond Calkins. He gave the first balcony window in memory of his parents, Joseph and Maria, and his sister, Martha, who died at the age of ten.

The studio of Reynolds, Francis and Rohnstock was commissioned to do the window. The firm was well known for its Gothic Revival designs, and the *Bancroft Window* is the earliest example of that style at First Church. The name of the studio appears at the lower edge of the stained glass. It is the church's only signed window.

The architectural firm of Allen and Collens assisted Bancroft in choosing the design. The three-lancet window, with each lancet bearing the name of one of those memorialized, has a grisaille background with an angel in the center panel. The overall geometric pattern painted with stylized foliage is characteristic of grisaille glass. A quatrefoil motif outlined in red is an integral part of the design and echoes a shape seen in other parts of the church.

[6] Mary of Bethany

DATE: 1957
STUDIO: The Willet Stained Glass Studios, Inc.
DEDICATION: Elizabeth Emma Morrill
DONOR: The Wednesday Informal Group

There was a twenty-eight-year hiatus between the installation of the *Bancroft Window* and the next windows installed in 1957. In that year, two windows were added in the chancel, and two on the east wall of the balcony. All of these Gothic Revival windows were designed by the Willet Studios of Philadelphia.

The Mary of Bethany theme was not a new one for First Church. The *Horsford Rose Window,* given by Phoebe Gardiner Horsford, also featured Mary.

The donor of the Willet window, the Wednesday Informal Group (WIGS), was organized by 1945. The women's organization provided support to a number of different groups and individuals, such as American Indian families, a minister's family in Nebraska, and the Boston Seaman's Friend Society. The WIGS raised money through a variety of activities, including cookbook and rummage sales.

Elizabeth Emma Morrill was one of the original members of the WIGS. When she died in 1955 at age forty-three, the women's group decided to make a permanent gift to the church in her memory. Though the group considered giving two windows, it was the Morrill family who eventually contributed the second window. *Dorcas* was given in memory of Grace Morrill, the mother of Elizabeth.

Three stained glass studios were considered by the WIGS: Willet, Connick, and Reynolds, Francis and Rohnstock. By March of 1956, the Willet Studios had been chosen. While E. Crosby Willet was responsible for suggesting the subject for both *Mary of Bethany* and *Dorcas,* it was Marguerite Gaudin who designed the windows. Two schemes were submitted for the WIGS' consideration. The women's group then made suggestions to the Willet Studios, including elimination of a third figure from one of the windows.

Mary of Bethany and *Dorcas* are similar in design. There is a three-part composition with a symbol in the upper section, a center area featuring the principal subject, and a decorative lower panel. The background is composed of blue and red glass with columns behind the figures. E. Crosby Willet suggested the Christian lamp of knowledge for the upper panel of *Mary of Bethany.* Interestingly, it appears as a lantern rather than as the more traditional oil lamp.

The Willet Studios, like Reynolds, Francis and Rohnstock, specialized in Gothic Revival glass. The windows are made of "antique," handmade but not necessarily old, glass to give them a medieval appearance. The primary colors, extensive painting on glass, and medieval look of the windows are a marked contrast to the earth colors and minimal enameling of earlier, opalescent windows.

[10] Dorcas

DATE: 1957
STUDIO: The Willet Stained Glass Studios, Inc.
DEDICATION: Grace Anderson Morrill
DONOR: Walter C. Morrill and John Anderson Morrill

Dorcas, along with angels and the Good Shepherd, was one of the most popular stained glass themes in the United States in both the nineteenth and twentieth centuries. Dorcas was a woman disciple from Joppa known for her generosity and charitable deeds. Two other Dorcas windows can be seen in Boston at the Church of the Covenant and Trinity Church.

While E. Crosby Willet chose the window subject, Marguerite Gaudin is credited with the window design. Ms. Gaudin joined the Willet Studios in 1931. She had designed stained glass in the Gothic Revival style for many well known churches and cathedrals, including the Cathedral of St. John the Divine in New York City and the Washington Cathedral in Washington, D.C.

Dorcas is shown giving a garment she has sewn to a young child. The figure in the background is a widow whom Dorcas has also assisted, according to the Willet Studios. When a cartoon of the window was submitted to the Wednesday Informal Group, which had originally commissioned the window, the members requested that "Dorcas's head be straightened." The symbol in the upper panel is a spool of thread and a needle, an appropriate motif for Dorcas.

Dorcas was given in memory of Grace Anderson Morrill by her husband, Walter C. Morrill, and her son, John Anderson Morrill.

Details of chancel windows designed by Marguerite Gaudin, showing the needle, thread, and scissors as a symbol for Dorcas, and the lamp of knowledge as a symbol for Mary of Bethany.

[18] Lester Grisaille Windows

DATE: 1957
STUDIO: The Willet Stained Glass Studios, Inc.
DEDICATIONS: To All Fathers and Mothers; To All Who Minister; To All Sons; To All Daughters
DONOR: Mary Ellis Purcell Lester

The Lester windows represent another variation on the grisaille theme. John A. Kevorkian of the Willet Studios, a photographer and portrait painter as well as a stained glass artist, is responsible for their design.

Mary E.P. Lester, the donor, consulted a number of studios, including the John Hardman Studios in Birmingham, England, and Reynolds, Francis and Rohnstock in Boston, before deciding on the Willet firm of Philadelphia. She studied historic grisaille patterns before submitting two drawings to the studio. Her first choice was an ivy pattern and her second, an acorn and oak leaf design. The final result was a variation on the latter theme.

Mrs. Lester submitted specifications to the Willet Studios regarding the design and construction of the windows. The studio was instructed to furnish "ornamental grisaille windows of artistic and intrinsic value equal to or greater than Bancroft in situ." In addition, "the window will be thoroughly staunch and weathertight, strongly barred and leaded." Mrs. Lester further specified that "all painted portions (are) to be fused in the kiln a sufficient number of times to render them absolutely fadeless as the work of the medieval glass artists which has stood the test of centuries." She requested that "the choicest hand-blown pot metal glasses" be used throughout with no cathedral, opalescent glasses or enamels. All the work was to be done freehand, rather than stenciled, and there was to be "no gauge cutting."

One of the primary concerns of Mrs. Lester was the relocation of the St. Catherine window, which was situated between the Lester windows. She felt that it was "out of place" and wished to have it moved to the Parish House. She was advised against doing so by the consultants Burnham and Skinner. Mrs. Lester specified that the Catherine window was not to be duplicated in any way and that she preferred something "more acceptable" with no figures, like the "jewel toned" windows on the north wall of the balcony. She suggested that something similar to the *Bancroft Window* would be surest to "please everybody and surest to offend nobody now or in the foreseeable future."

There are both similarities and differences between the Bancroft and the Lester windows. They both utilize a quatrefoil motif, bright red and blue glass, and a medieval look. The *Lester Grisaille Windows*, however, contain more clear glass, greater color variation, different design motifs, and lack a human figure.

The use of silver stain is apparent in the Lester windows. Silver salts were applied to some areas of the glass, making a permanent stain of yellow. The result is sections of silver color on the exterior and yellow detailing on the interior of the glass.

Each of the four lancets has both a general dedication and the name or names of members of Mrs. Lester's family. The window honoring fathers and mothers bears the names of Mrs. Lester's parents, William Beckes Purcell and Mary Dorcas McCord Purcell. Another window dedicated to "All who Minister" bears the name of her sister, Mabel Clare Purcell Clarke. There are two windows honoring sons and daughters. One window bears her son's name, William Purcell Lester, and the other, her daughter's name, Louise Horatia Lester Wing.

[17] Christ Blessing Little Children

DATE: 1957
STUDIO: The Willet Stained Glass Studios, Inc.
DEDICATION: To Little Children Everywhere
DONOR: Mary Ellis Purcell Lester

In addition to the grisaille windows, Mary Lester commissioned the Willet Studios to execute a design for the oculus window in the balcony. John Kevorkian was the designer of that window as well.

At the dedication of the Willet chancel and balcony windows in 1957, Dr. Henry Lee Willet emphasized the value of stained glass. He believed that windows helped one to worship and that the appropriate glass was pot metal or colored glass, in contrast to streaky, opalescent glass. He further commented that "the window should be two dimensional and decorative, following, but not copying, the great tradition of the medieval stained glass artists whose windows have stood as inspiration to worshippers for eight hundred years or more."

The oculus window reflects a number of design elements that are present in earlier windows. For example, there is a quatrefoil motif which is part of both the Bancroft and the Lester grisaille stained glass. In addition, the setting, with the suggestion of a colonnade in the background, is very similar to the two Willet Gothic Revival windows in the apse.

The following words are incorporated into the window: "To Little Children Everywhere" and "For the descendants of Horace Hardy Lester and Mary Ellis Purcell Lester."

At one time, the Wednesday Informal Group provided lighting for the window so that it was visible from the outside at night. Mrs. Lester expressed her appreciation to the women's group, commenting, "It is not too much to suppose that a single sudden sight of this silent, softly shining symbol of your devotion to God and to humanity may, upon occasion, restrain those who plan evil or restore those distraught by awareness of the evil about them. The constantly recurring sight of it will be a true benediction."

[20] Chapel Windows

DATE: C. 1939
STUDIO: Arthur Murray Dallin

The stained glass artist Arthur Murray Dallin designed the three lancet *Chapel Windows*. The three sections are identical and are composed of diamond-shaped glass pieces painted with fired mattes. The window probably dates from the time of the chapel's completion in 1939. The names of the two major benefactors of the chapel, Edwin Parker Lindsay and Agnes Morton Lindsay, are incorporated into the lower part of the windows.

The artist, Arthur Dallin, apprenticed at the Connick Studio in Boston, later worked for Earl E. Sanborn, and then opened his own studio in 1932. The First Church *Chapel Windows* were completed about seven years later.

Additional Windows

[*] SMALL STENCILED LUNETTES

The seven small lunettes, which are operable vents, are composed of stenciled quarries with antique glass borders. Glass pieces have been replaced over the years. The windows date from either the late nineteenth or early twentieth century.

[5] & [11]
OPALESCENT CHANCEL WINDOWS

The provenance and date of the two end chancel windows is unknown. Like the three other opalescent windows in the chancel, these two windows are divided into three sections. There is a design motif in the upper section, a center area with a suggestion of columns at the edge, and a lower panel. In the upper section of number five is an alpha symbol, and in number eleven, omega. Unlike the other opalescent chancel windows, the middle sections of the two end windows lack figures, and there are no inscriptions in the lower panels.

Opalescent Chancel Windows are pictured in their entirety on pp. 4 and 5

Glossary

ANTIQUE GLASS: mouth-blown glass made by the muff method, in which a tube of glass is blown, then split lengthwise and opened to create a rectangular sheet

APSE: a semicircular or polygonal, usually domed projection of a building, especially at the altar end of a church

CARTOON: a fullsize drawing for a window design

CATHEDRAL GLASS: machine-rolled clear or colored glass

CHANCEL: the area around the altar of a church, often enclosed by a railing

DRAPERY GLASS: opalescent glass that is manipulated during its manufacture to form folds similar in appearance to cloth

ENAMEL: opaque, colored glass paint made essentially from powdered, colored glass

GRISAILLE: 1. black, brown, grey, or other dark vitreous paint used to decorate glass 2. windows of ornamental design decorated primarily with this paint, using little or no colored glass

LANCET: a tall, narrow window opening

LUNETTE: a semicircular window

MATTE PAINT: washes of glass paint, usually grisaille, typically applied to the interior surface of the glass and used for shading

NAVE: the central part of a church, extending from the narthex to the chancel and flanked by aisles

OCULUS: a circular window not divided by spokes or radii

OPALESCENT GLASS: milky, opaque glass, often of more than one color, developed by late nineteenth century American glassmakers for Louis Comfort Tiffany and John La Farge

PREDELLA: the step or platform upon which the altar stands

QUARRY: geometric shapes of glass used in a repeating design

QUATREFOIL: an ornament or tracery with four equal foils or lobes

ROSE WINDOW: a circular window divided by radial mullions, usually in a floral or wheel pattern

SEDILIA: a set of seats, generally three, built into the wall of the south side of the choir near the altar in Gothic style churches for use by the celebrant and the ministers

SILVER STAIN: a type of paint composed of silver nitrate or silver chloride applied to the exterior surface of glass; when fired, it stains the glass a yellow to golden-orange color

TRACERY: lacy openwork in a window

VITREOUS PAINT: paint composed of ground glass and metallic oxide pigments, fired in a kiln to melt and fuse with the surface of the glass; it is applied to glass for detailing and enhancement

Donors and Dedications

Windows are listed in chronological order.

[3] Horsford Rose Window, 1872
Dedication: Mary L'Hommedieu Gardiner Horsford
Donor: Phoebe Gardiner Horsford

[8] The Good Shepherd, 1894
Dedication: Dedicated to the work of young women in the Church
Donor: The Shepard Guild

[4] The Four Elements, 1895
Dedication: Phoebe Gardiner Horsford and Eben Norton Horsford
Bequest: Eben Norton Horsford

[2] They Shall Be Mine, Saith the Lord, 1895
Dedication: Mary Horsford Curtis
Donor: Phoebe Gardiner Horsford

[7] Fuller Window, 1895
Dedication: Harriet Maria Fuller and her son, Charles Richard Fuller
Donor: Unknown

[9] Angel, 1895
Dedication: Alexander McKenzie
Donor: The Nevertheless Circle of King's Daughters

[14] Resurrection Angel, 1897
Dedication: Alexander McKenzie's Thirty Years of Service to First Church
Donor: Friends of Alexander McKenzie

[15] St. Paul, 1898
Dedication: Charles Theodore Russell
Donor: Sarah Elizabeth Russell

[1] Faith, 1898
Dedication: Sarah Elizabeth Russell
Donor: Russell sons: Charles, Joseph, and Henry

[12] Hart Window, 1901
Dedication: Horace Putnam Hart
Donor: Professor and Mrs. Albert Bushnell Hart

[19] St. Catherine of Alexandria, 1908
Dedication: Martha Theresa Fiske
Donor: Mr. and Mrs. Josiah M. Fiske

[13] Kimball/Rice Window, 1918, 1960
Dedication of center panel and tracery windows: Harriet T. Neally Kimball
Bequest: W. Frederick Kimball
Dedication of two side lancets: "To the Glory of God and the Service of His Church"
Donor: Mr. and Mrs. Frederick A. Rice

[16] Bancroft Window, 1929
Dedication: Joseph, Maria, and Martha Bancroft
Donor: Jacob Bancroft

[6] Mary of Bethany, 1957
Dedication: Elizabeth Emma Morrill
Donor: The Wednesday Informal Group

[10] Dorcas, 1957
Dedication: Grace Anderson Morrill
Donor: Walter C. Morrill and John Anderson Morrill

[18] Lester Grisaille Windows, 1957
Dedication: To All Fathers and Mothers, To All Sons, To All Daughters, and To All Who Minister. Specific dedications on each of four window sections to Mary E.P. Lester's parents, sister, son, and daughter.
Donor: Mary Ellis Purcell Lester

[17] Christ Blessing Little Children, 1957
Dedication: To Little Children Everywhere; For the descendants of Horace Hardy Lester and Mary Ellis Purcell Lester
Donor: Mary Ellis Purcell Lester

[20] Chapel Windows, c. 1939
The names of Edwin Parker Lindsay and Agnes Morton Lindsay, the major benefactors of the chapel, are incorporated into the lower part of the windows.

Ministers

First Church in Cambridge, Congregational

1633–1636	Thomas Hooker
1636–1649	Thomas Shepard
1650–1668	Jonathan Mitchell
1671–1682	Urian Oakes
1682–1692	Nathaniel Gookin
1696–1717	William Brattle
1717–1783	Nathaniel Appleton
1783–1790	Timothy Hilliard
1792–1831	Abiel Holmes
1831–1834	Nehemiah Adams
1835–1867	John A. Albro
1867–1912	Alexander McKenzie
1912–1940	Raymond Calkins
1940–1962	John H. Leamon
1962–1976	Wells B. Grogan
1977–	Allen Happe

Stained Glass Studios

The following are brief profiles of the stained glass studios and architectural firms that have contributed to First Church's continually evolving design. Besides charting the often frequent name changes, these sketches provide short histories of the studios and firms as well as biographical information about individual designers.

1879	L.C. Tiffany & Associated Artists, New York City
1885	The Tiffany Glass Company Incorporated, New York City
1890	The Tiffany Glass & Decorating Company, New York City
1900	Tiffany Studios, New York City
1932	Tiffany Studios files for bankruptcy

Louis Comfort Tiffany (1848–1933) was the son of a well-known New York jeweler, Charles Lewis Tiffany. The young Tiffany attended boarding school and later studied at the National Academy of Design in New York City. He was interested in both watercolor and oil painting and studied with two well-known artists of the time, George Inness and Samuel Coleman.

By the 1870s, Tiffany and another artist, John La Farge, were experimenting with different kinds of glass. The result was an entirely new form of glass, now called opalescent. By the 1890s, the Tiffany firm had nearly cornered the stained glass market, and the name "Tiffany" became virtually synonymous with American stained glass.

Tiffany windows can be found throughout the United States; in Massachusetts alone there are well over 200 Tiffany examples. In addition to First Church, the following churches have one or more Tiffany windows:

- Church of the Covenant, Boston
- Arlington Street Church, Boston
- Christ Episcopal Church, Fitchburg
- North Congregational Church, Haverhill
- St. Anne's Episcopal Church, Lowell
- St. John's Episcopal Church, North Adams
- First Congregational Church, North Adams
- The Eliot Congregational Church, Roxbury

1888–1897	Phipps, Slocum and Company, Boston
1898–1918	Horace J. Phipps and Company, Boston
1919–1922	Phipps, Ball and Burnham Company, Brighton
1923– ?	Horace J. Phipps, Boston

Stained glass examples from some of the above studios can be seen in the following churches as well as at First Church:

- Second Presbyterian Church, Portsmouth, Ohio
- Cathedral of St. John, Denver, Colorado

1923–1953	Reynolds, Francis and Rohnstock, Boston
1954–1964	Joseph G. Reynolds and Associates, Boston

Joseph G. Reynolds was born in Wickford, Rhode Island and graduated from the Rhode Island School of Design in 1907. In 1923, Reynolds, William H. Francis, and J. Henry Rohnstock started their own business. Reynolds was the director and designer, Francis, the glass painter, and Rohnstock, the foreman of the glaziers and cutters. All three members of the firm were formerly associated with the Connick Studio in Boston. After the death of Reynolds's two partners, the studio name was changed to Joseph G. Reynolds and Associates.

In addition to the windows at First Church, Reynolds, Francis and Rohnstock stained glass can be seen at the following locations:

- The Cathedral of St. John the Divine, New York City
- Saint Bartholomew's Church, New York City
- Riverside Church, New York City
- Houghton Memorial Chapel, Wellesley College, Wellesley, Massachusetts
- Princeton University Chapel, Princeton, New Jersey
- Washington Cathedral, Washington, D.C.
- The American Church, Paris, France
- The American Memorial Cemetery Chapel, Belleau Wood, Belleau, France

---

The Willet Stained Glass Studios, Inc.

William Willet (1867–1921) was born in New York City. He studied with William Merritt Chase and at The Mechanics and Tradesmen's Institute, now Cooper Union. Willet was associated with a number of stained glass studios, including that of John La Farge in 1885. By 1897, he and his wife, Anne Lee Willet, had established their own studio, first in Pittsburgh and later in Philadelphia.

After William Willet's death, the studio continued under the direction of his widow and their son, Henry Lee Willet (1899–1983). Henry was educated at Princeton University and the Wharton School of Business. He became president of the firm in 1930.

E. Crosby Willet (1928–), Henry's son, has carried on the family tradition, becoming president of the studio in 1964. In 1977, ownership of the firm was transferred to the Hauser Glass Studio of Winona, Minnesota.

In addition to the examples at First Church, Willet windows can be seen at the following locations:

- Washington Hall and Chapel, U.S. Military Academy, West Point, New York
- Washington Cathedral, Washington, D.C.
- Cathedral of St. John the Divine, New York City
- Princeton University Chapel, Princeton, New Jersey
- Chapel Center at the United Nations, New York City

Arthur Murray Dallin

Arthur M. Dallin (1897–1940), the son of sculptor Cyrus E. Dallin, was born in France, where his father was studying at the École des Beaux-Arts. The Dallin family later returned to the United States. A.M. Dallin graduated from the Arlington High School and went on to study at the Boston Museum School. He apprenticed with both the Connick Studio and the Earl E. Sanborn Studios before opening his own stained glass business in Arlington, Massachusetts.

Dallin designed windows for more than fifty churches in the United States, among them St. Luke's Parish in Belmont and First Church in Cambridge, Congregational.

In addition to a career in stained glass design, Dallin had a distinguished military career. He joined the French forces at the beginning of the First World War, serving with an ambulance unit. He was awarded the Croix de Guerre for distinguished service during that war.

Dallin returned to France in 1939, along with some friends who had also fought in the First World War, and rejoined the French forces. In 1940, German troops entered the Department of Aisne and captured the Twelfth Regiment, of which Dallin was a member. He died at Luzancy-Sur-Marne on June 12. He was awarded the Medaille Militaire, the highest decoration bestowed on a French soldier.

Architects

While Abel C. Martin designed the original church structure in 1871, significant modifications were made in later years by other architects. The firm of Allen and Collens was responsible for a major renovation of the sanctuary in 1924, and William H. McLean designed an addition to the church two years later. Harold B. Willis is credited with the redesign of the steeple in 1938 and the interior design of the chapel in 1939. The central liturgical area in the sanctuary was designed by Perry K. Neubauer of The Architects Collaborative in 1972.

1866–1868	Abel C. Martin and S.J.F. Thayer
1869	Abel C. Martin and W.P.P. Longfellow
1870–1879	Abel C. Martin

Abel C. Martin (1835–1879) graduated from Harvard's Scientific School in 1856. His undergraduate training was in engineering, and he joined the architectural firm of Arthur Gilman shortly after his graduation.

Martin designed a variety of buildings, including hotels, churches, schools, and private residences. He was particularly interested in and wrote frequently about building ventilation, especially in regard to schools.

A member of the American Institute of Architects, Martin was one of the founders of the Boston Society of Architects.

The details of his untimely death were chronicled in an 1879 issue of *The American Architect and Building News:*

He was driving home with one of his clients after a professional consultation when an accident occurred at a drawbridge which they were about to cross, and Mr. Martin, getting down from the carriage was run over by a frightened horse, and received injuries from which he died four or five days later.

The following are some examples of Martin's work in Massachusetts:

- Trinity Methodist Church, Cambridge
- First Church in Cambridge, Congregational, Cambridge
- George Upton residence, Boston
- Chauncy Hall School, Boston
- Office Building, Boston
- Bowditch School, Salem
- Park Theater, Boston

1903–1933	Allen and Collens
1934–1939	Allen, Collens and Willis
1940–1942	Collens, Willis and Hubbard
1942–1962	Collens, Willis and Beckonert

Both Francis R. Allen (1843–1931) and Charles Collens (1873–1956) received prestigious architectural educations. Allen graduated from Amherst College and went on to study architecture at both M.I.T. and the École des Beaux-Arts in Paris. Collens was a graduate of Yale University and also studied at the École des Beaux-Arts.

The firm of Allen and Collens had a national reputation and was a leading exponent of the Neo-Gothic style.

The following are just a few of Allen and Collens's commissions:

- State Street Bank, Boston
- Memorial Chapel, Union Theological Seminary, New York
- Andover Hall, Harvard Divinity School, Cambridge
- Second Church, Newton
- St. Clements Church, Boston
- Sanctuary renovation, First Church in Cambridge, Congregational, Cambridge

- Lindsey Memorial Chapel, Emmanuel Church, Boston
- Newton City Hall, Newton

Harold Buckley Willis (1890–1962), a Harvard graduate, joined the firm of Allen and Collens shortly after the First World War. He became a partner in the firm in 1934. Willis participated in the design of buildings at Mt. Holyoke College, Springfield College, and Newton City Hall. At First Church, he was responsible for the redesign of the steeple in 1938 and the interior of the chapel in 1939.

Willis's wartime experiences were dramatic enough to be chronicled in obituaries in both the *Boston Herald* and *The New York Times*. In World War I, Willis was officially declared dead after his airplane was shot down in 1917. In fact, he was captured behind enemy lines in Verdun, France and placed in the first of a series of ten German prison camps. Just before the Armistice, he escaped and swam across the Rhine River, making his way to the Swiss frontier and freedom. In World War II, Willis served in the Army Air Force, retiring with the rank of colonel.

After the Second World War, Willis returned to his architectural practice and remained active until his death in 1962.

1901	William H. McLean
1902–1911	McLean and Wright
1912–1917	McLean (William H.) and McLean (Henry)
1918–1938	William H. McLean

William H. McLean (1870–1942) practiced architecture in New England for more than thirty years. At the time of his death in 1942, he was a resident of Middleboro, Massachusetts.

The following are some examples of McLean's work:

- Provincetown High School, Provincetown, Massachusetts
- Bellows Free Academy, St. Albans, Vermont
- Library, North Attleboro, Massachusetts
- Addition, First Church in Cambridge, Congregational, Cambridge, Massachusetts

1940–	Perry K. Neubauer

Graduating with honors from Princeton University in 1962, Perry K. Neubauer subsequently received two degrees from the Harvard Graduate School of Design, a Bachelor of Architecture in 1964 and a Master of Architecture in Urban Design in 1965. Associated since 1965 with the prominent Cambridge architectural firm, The Architects Collaborative, Inc., he is president and a principal of that firm.

The following are just a few of Neubauer's many noteworthy architectural and planning design projects:

- School of Business, University of Wisconsin, Madison, Wisconsin
- Egyptian Museum Renovation, Cairo, Egypt
- National Library and Cultural Center, Abu Dhabi, United Arab Emirates
- Performing Arts Center, Virginia Commonwealth University, Richmond, Virginia
- Plymouth Congregational Church, Plymouth, New Hampshire
- Master Plan for Jubail Industrial City, Jubail, Saudi Arabia
- Comprehensive and Long Range Plan for Capitol Center, Tallahassee, Florida
- Hotel Bernardin, Piran, Yugoslavia
- Cross, communion table, and baptismal font, First Church in Cambridge, Congregational, Cambridge, Massachusetts

Bibliography

Adams, Henry. *Mont Saint-Michel and Chartres.* New York, 1985.

Archives of American Art, Smithsonian Institution. Reynolds, Francis and Rohnstock papers.

Arlington Advocate. Arlington, Massachusetts, 1940, 1946.

Boston Public Library. Fine Arts Department. Architectural files.

Boston Public Library. Microtext Department. Newspaper files.

Buttrick, George, ed. *The Interpreter's Dictionary of the Bible.* New York, 1962.

Calkins, Raymond. *The Life and Times of Alexander McKenzie.* Cambridge, 1935.

Cambridge Chronicle. Cambridge, 1871–1960.

Cambridge Directories. Cambridge, 1871–1960.

Cambridge Historical Commission. *Survey of Architectural History in Cambridge.* Reports 1–5. Cambridge, 1965, 1967, 1971, 1973, 1977.

Cambridge Tribune. Cambridge, 1878–1941.

Chamberlain, Joseph. "The First Church in Cambridge, Congregational: Some Events in Its Life." *Cambridge Historical Society Proceedings.* Vol. 43, pp. 111–126, Cambridge, 1980.

Coe, Brian. *Stained Glass in England 1150–1550.* London, 1981.

Connick, Charles. *Adventures in Light and Color: An Introduction to the Stained Glass Craft.* New York, 1937.

Duncan, Alastair. *Tiffany Windows.* New York, 1982.

First Church in Cambridge, Congregational. Archives.

Harvard University. Archives.

Koch, Robert. *Louis C. Tiffany, Rebel in Glass.* New York, 1966.

Lee, Lawrence et al. *Stained Glass.* New York, 1976.

McKean, Hugh F. *The "Lost" Treasures of Louis Comfort Tiffany.* New York, 1980.

McKenzie, Alexander. *First Church in Cambridge.* Boston, 1873.

Mount Auburn Cemetery. Archives.

Paige, Lucius R. *History of Cambridge, Massachusetts, 1630–1877 with a Genealogical Register.* Boston, 1877.

Strong, James. *Strong's Exhaustive Concordance of the Bible.* New York, 1977.

Sturm, James, and James Chotas. *Stained Glass from Medieval Times to the Present.* New York, 1982.

The Charles Hosmer Morse Foundation, Inc. Archives.

The Holy Bible. Authorized King James version.

The Second Reformed Church, Hackensack, New Jersey. Archives.

The Willet Stained Glass Studios, Inc., Philadelphia, Pennsylvania. Archives.

Design: Susan Marsh

Type Composition: DEKR Corporation

Printing: Mercantile Printing Company